Small Business Fraud
101 Lessons From Embezzlers

Allan F. Hambleton

Presented by Success Track® Training

It is recommended that if you suspect an employee of fraud or embezzlement in your place or work, do not attempt to investigate on your own, but obtain the services of a professional in this field. Such a professional can be a Certified Fraud Examiner or Certified Public Accountant.

This book is written from actual embezzlement case experience. If the things mentioned in this book are permitted in your organization, then you are running the risk of having embezzlement in your business operations.

The writer does not intend to teach anyone how to commit fraud but rather has written this book to help owners and managers avoid being ripped off by fraud and embezzlement.

This book is not intended to cause mental, psychological or emotional damage to anyone. This is why the names of businesses and embezzlement perpetrators' names have not been used. Also, everyone is responsible for their own actions. The author and the publisher are not rendering any legal, psychological or adverse advice by what is written herein.

Preface

Employed embezzlers discover many different ways to rip off their employers. This is what is fascinating about this business - discovering how someone did it! But it is usually a repeat of the same thing using a different method. Embezzlement could be defeated if certain principles were administered and adhered to throughout the life of a business. Embezzlers do not have much mercy on their employer when it comes to stealing another person's money. They have their own problems to cope with such as gambling, drugs or some other addiction; or, they may have resentment toward their employer for some reason. Employers should not show mercy when trying to discover potential fraud and embezzlements. The person, when found out, should face the full force of the law. If they do not, the chances are that they will do it again sometime in the future and put another employer through the same type of grief that you went through. Please read this book with care and don't think it can't happen to you or to your business or your department. You could lose your business over a fraud or embezzlement. You could lose your reputation over it as well. The resultant consequences could be devastating to you and your family. Many a family has already experienced such difficulties. Some have had to mortgage their homes to meet payroll or to pay bills. This book is written in an easy to understand format - these are actual lessons learned from the embezzlers themselves. Under each lesson you will find a recommendation to avoid the problem. The lessons are the result of years of study on this topic. Most of them are in the realm of common sense - but employers do not use many of these principles. Utilize the recommendations given in this book and you will not have to face the same traumas that have plagued others. Don't let this happen to you. Save your business. Be one step ahead of the embezzlers. Learn from *101 Lessons from Embezzlers*.

Allan F. Hambleton, MBA, CMA,
Associate, Certified Fraud Examiners Association.
5 March, 2017.

Contents

Definitions of Embezzlement

"To steal (money) that belongs to the company or organization that one works for."

Collins Dictionary

"The fraudulent appropriation of property by a person to whom it has been entrusted; as, the embezzlement by a clerk of his employer's; embezzlement of public funds by the public officer having them in charge."

Webster's Dictionary

"Theft or misappropriation of funds placed in one's trust or belonging to one's employer."

Oxford Dictionary

1 Accounting

Lesson 1. Don't ignore accounting backlogs.

Accounting backlogs are a breeding ground for fraud and embezzlement. If the books are not up to date start asking questions "why?" If you can't tell what is going on this should make you very nervous. How would you know that you are not being ripped off? It could be months before you could find out even if you bring in an expert to fix it all. By then the bookkeeper could be gone and far away with your money.

Recommendation: Ensure that all major aspects of accounting are up to date. This would include the bank reconciliations, the general ledger postings and the bank deposits.

Lesson 2. Don't ignore the need for double verification on every financial item.

Some employers have learned this lesson the hard way. Take for example a farming operation to put all their confidence in an embezzling bookkeeper. She took the accounts payable checks to the boss for signature and then took them back to her desk only to add her name to the payee line: "[Vendor] ... or Mary Smith' If the employer had double verification in place before the checks left the office this would not have happened and he still would have had his million dollars.

Recommendation: Check and double check every accounting transaction. You never leave anyone on their own in charge of so many vital activities.

Lesson 3. Don't avoid double entry accounting principle is used.

Accounting is set up with double entries for a reason and that reason is to keep the books in balance. Any time a one sided journal is used there is potential danger. The double entry system ensures that all the debits equal all the credits. This ensures balance in the books.

Recommendation: Never permit a one sided accounting entry. You will be inviting trouble if you do not keep an eye on this. The double entry system is a safety check on the business accounting and its use is meant to help prevent embezzlement. It is a top priority to ensure the system is running correctly.

Lesson 4. Don't avoid checking all postings to the general ledger.

When a person commits embezzlement it is nearly always recorded somehow in the general ledger. Look for unusual things posted such as excessive costs in one category or another. You can compare previous year's costs with current year costs to see if there is much variation.

Recommendation: By not checking all postings to the general ledger you run the risk of having bogus entries posted.

For example, you could have someone steals from you and then post it to the general ledger as a regular expense.

2 Afford

Lesson 5. Don't allow "we can't afford it" to make ill - advised decisions.

Some employers don't think they can afford the cost of checking out potential employees and hire the first person who comes along with apparent qualifications. Other employers don't think they can afford to hire a suitably qualified individual to do the job and pay for it later.

Recommendation: Spend a reasonable amount of money to do the job correctly. It costs money but it can cost you a whole lot more in embezzled funds. Don't take chances with things like hiring the right person, paying for the right labor and so on.

Lesson 6. Don't allow person who collects receivables to perform aging.

When bookkeepers collect receivables (payments on account) they can divert the funds to their own use. They can do this by opening up a bank account in a similar name to your company and depositing the revenues. So if they also have the responsibility for aging receivables they can adjust them to make it appear that the customer has paid or just leave them off altogether.

Recommendation: This may cost extra money but it is well worth it. It will take segregation of duties - but an important segregation of duties. Ensure that you have enough employees to cover this situation. You should segregate the following activities:

1. Receiving payments for work done or goods sold;

2. Recording the receipt of funds;

3. Making up the bank deposit, and

4. Taking the bank deposit to the bank.

3   Always Done it That Way

Lesson 7. Don't allow "we have always done it this way" to exist.

When permission is given by default or otherwise to continue things that are done because they have always been done that way, the employer is inviting potential problems. One woman always asked for money to pay for clients and yet no clients were seen in her area. But since it was always done that way it was not questioned.

Recommendation: Question everything, never accept the status quo. The status quo could be wrong and could send you to the bankruptcy attorney. Always ask questions - why do they do it that way?

4   Annual Audit

Lesson 8. Don't avoid having an audit.

Audits are important even for small companies. They can locate and discover certain frauds and an auditor will know what to do about it. Some companies don't have an audit because they say they can't afford it.

Recommendation: But a company cannot afford not to have an audit. If you are concerned about cost go out to bid. Make sure the auditors are qualified to do the job.

Lesson 9. Don't think that an annual audit makes you fraud - free.

Don't think that because you have an audit each year that you are fraud free. This could not be further from the truth. Many companies have discovered fraud through ways other than audits. Other employees have often been a big help in uncovering embezzlement. Auditors focus on the big picture when it is the little things that can be important.

Recommendation: Listen to your employees. They sometimes will be able to put their finger on a problem when the auditors were not. Don't give up on being alert to fraud just because you have had an auditor.

Lesson 10. Don't avoid putting into practice the auditor's recommendations.

Auditor's recommendations should be implemented. They are usually recommendations to shore up internal control weaknesses. They are meant to avoid future problems such as fraud.

Recommendation: Some of these recommendations may be difficult for a business to implement but the staff should be instructed to implement them and told to report back to you (the owner / manager) when they are done. A letter should go to the audit firm telling them when they are finalized.

5 Assets

Lesson 11. Don't avoid a register of valuable, attractive and important assets.

You must have a register of valuable and attractive assets such as laptop computers. Some of these have gone missing over the years and are probably in employees' homes or have been sold by employees. Just recently a major company in the US lost millions of dollars over its IT Manager buying and then later selling the same purchases for his own benefit.

Recommendation: Have someone reliable put together a valuable assets register and a written policy to go with it. Try to establish the separation of duties when anyone has the power to buy. You should segregate the following activities:

1. The actual purchase of the product;

2. The receiving of the those products by another person; and,

3. The payment for those products purchased.

Lesson 12. Don't neglect having employees sign for assets taken.

When sign outs are absent that is when things go missing. Making employees accountable for their equipment loans is important because then you know who has taken what. State governments have learned this the hard way.

Recommendation: Have all employees sign out valuable assets when they are taken with no exceptions for management or, for example, the IT Manager. Have a valuable register custodian. Make sure this duty is given to someone reliable, someone who does the job the way it is specified. Make sure that they follow up on items that are not returned in a reasonable amount of time.

Lesson 13. Don't be ignorant to unauthorized company asset sales.

Keep your eye out for unauthorized asset sales - your assets. This has happened in companies and the funds go into the pockets of an unethical employee. What is to stop a "reputable" manager from selling your assets? It happened recently where an IT manager was buying assets and turning right around and selling them.

Recommendation: Always make employees accountable for assets. Have an assets register for every asset held in the organization and make someone independent of the operations (say in accounting) the custodian of such a register. Have that person do regular audits of equipment.

6 Banking

Lesson 14. Don't allow financial employees take signature cards to bank

One agency found out the hard way why you don't let employees take signature cards to the bank. Why? Because they can simply add their own name to the signature card and become a signatory to that account. If then they have opportunity to write a check they can without the bank questioning it.

Recommendation: Take all signature cards to the bank yourself. A fifteen minute chore is better than fighting to get your money back after you have been embezzled.

Lesson 15. Don't allow accounts receivable person to make up bank deposits

If this is done then the person responsible for accounts receivable can fabricate the records to make it look like a customer has paid but take the payment themselves. They can leave the payment out of the bank deposit and convert it to their own use. This is especially dangerous if management is relying upon this person to produce the aged receivable listing of accounts.

Recommendation: Get someone other than the accounts receivable person to make up the bank deposit.

Lesson 16. Don't allow banks to open accounts in the company name

You need to inform your bank that all bank accounts opened in the name of your business must be done only with your authority.

Recommendation: Write a letter to your bank not permitting any bank account to be opened in your or your business name without your authority.

Lesson 17. Don't allow an accounts payable employee to receive bank statements

This is very important since they can cover up what they have done if they receive the bank statements. The bank statements should be received by the owner of the business or the manager who should look then over for irregularities. This will also deter embezzlement if they are in the habit of doing this.

Recommendation: Get your bank to address the bank statements to you.

Lesson 18. Don't forget to close unused bank accounts

Some organizations have learned this lesson the hard way. One in particular lost over a million dollars this way. The embezzler received a refund check once a year from an association which he deposited in an unused bank account with his signature authorized. He was supposed to have closed this account about ten years before but did not.

Recommendation: Keep an eye out for all your bank accounts and close them personally if you have no further use for them.

7 Budget

Lesson 19. Don't neglect an annual budget

An annual budget indicates where you should be at any particular time of the year. Actual results should be compared to the budget to see if any expenses of revenues are that different to what was expected.

Recommendation: This is why it is important for a responsible person or owner to figure out the budget from the beginning - to do a zero based budget based upon expectations for the business operations rather than the actual results from last year.

8 Cash

Lesson 20. Don't ignore overall cash shortages when business is going well

Recently there was a case where the owners had to take mortgages on their homes due to a very large embezzlement. The owners had not taken enough notice of their cash position.

Recommendation: If your business is going well and you don't have enough cash something is wrong, right? Don't ignore your common sense regarding this.

Lesson 21. Don't permit employees to exchange checks for money orders

There is no reason to do this. So if anyone is doing this then something is generally wrong. One agency learned this lesson the hard way. Their CEO had an employee convert funds to money orders and then take them to his house.

Recommendation: Management overrides like this should not be permitted and should be investigated as soon as possible.

9   Checks

Lesson 22. Don't allow signed checks back to person who originated them.

I know of an employer who wishes he never did this. What is to stop the accounts payable bookkeeper taking the checks after they were signed and added their own name to the payee line or whiting out the name of the payee and putting in their own name? Don't allow this to happen.

Recommendation: Ensure that checks don't go back to the person who prepared them.

Lesson 23. Don't allow financial employees to sign checks.

There have been many employers who wished they never permitted this to occur. Even though it is sometimes a lot more difficult it is important that the owner or responsible manager sign all checks. Even Oprah still signs all her own checks.

Recommendation: Apparently the temptation to sign checks for fraudulent purposes can be too much for some people. Don't put temptation in anyone's path. Don't allow financial people to sign checks.

Lesson 24. Don't leave accounts payable checks unsecured.

A janitor once got hold of some checks that were left unattended and made out checks to himself and his relatives. Never discount the value of checks. Never leave them unattended or unsecured. They can disappear and no-one will know what happened to them until they hit the bank account.

Recommendation: Secure all checks under lock and key.

Lesson 25. Don't avoid doing sequence checks on check stock.

As part of securing checks an employer needs to ensure that sequence checks are done on checks from time to time. This will ensure that all checks are accounted for and none are missing. When someone steals company checks they normally take checks that are quite away ahead in numbers so as not to permit them to be noticed right away.

Recommendation: Do a regular sequence check on check stock to ensure that none are missing.

Lesson 26. Don't permit anyone to have their names printed on checks received.

One public agency did not put a stop to this and found out the hard way that this is the way for checks to be stolen. Sometimes vendors write people's contact name son checks.

Recommendation: If you find this is happening to anyone in your organization, **PUT A STOP TO IT**.

Lesson 27. Don't avoid checking the check register for voided checks.

Sometimes employees make mistakes on checks and they need to be voided by tearing off the signature place and keeping them in a special file.

Recommendation: Don't permit them to be destroyed since then you have no evidence that they were in fact destroyed. They should be kept securely in a locked cabinet or vault.

Lesson 28. Don't ignore need for two signatures on checks if owner can't sign.

It is best to have the owner sign all checks as previously mentioned. But if he or she cannot do this then two signatures should be insisted upon for every check. Some embezzlements have occurred when only one signature was required.

Recommendation: Two signatures on an account and therefore on checks, although not a fool-proof system, generally requires collusion to embezzle.

Lesson 29. Don't forget to install positive pay into accounts payable system.

Some banks offer positive pay. That is, they won't permit any check to be taken off the account without prior notification by the business entity. This is a good way to avoid having unauthorized checks taken off your bank account.

Recommendation: Contact your bank and see if they offer this service. If they do not offer this service, then change banks.

10 Claims

Lesson 30. Don't assume that all claims paid against the firm are valid.

Don't assume that since you have received claims and are paying for them that they are always valid. Recently there was a case in a State Revenue Department where an auditor of many years employment history was caught making out false refunds to family names.

Recommendation: No matter how high up a person is they are still human and subject to temptation. Internal controls such as having a second unrelated person review all refunds is appropriate in all refund cases.

Lesson 31. Don't assume that all claims received are valid.

All claims received are not necessarily valid. Don't assume that they are just because they have been presented to you. There could be bogus claims sent to you, Beware of any rush claims that are presented.

Recommendation: Insist on copies of identification (ID) for the claimant, for example, passport and credit card and driver's license. Ensure that all names match.

11 Collusion

Lesson 32. Don't think collusion cannot happen in your firm.

A water district found out the hard way that collusion can and does sometimes raise its ugly head. Several employees were found to have colluded on this fraud. They were buying parts at exorbitant prices from a fraud-included supplier. It was an employee who raised the alarm on this one.

Recommendation: Although this is rare it does happen occasionally. Make embezzlement reporting profitable and rewarding for those who may want to do it.

12 Common Sense

Lesson 33. Don't turn a blind eye to common sense.

Sometimes common sense occurs to our application of our business. Things just don't make sense or seem unusual. Don't ignore the obvious. Don't ignore what does seem right in your business. It maybe slowly slipping away from you into another's hands.

Recommendation: Don't ignore the warning signs and that sixth sense you have to problems. Investigate where your gut feel is heading.

13　Complacency

Lesson 34. Don't think if there is no fraud now that you won't have it eventually.

Sometimes employers get complacent and because an embezzlement has not occurred in their history (that they know anyway) it probably will not happen. I have had employers shirk their responsibility to this. One in particular said if you can't trust people then you might as well not be in business. This is not true. It's that people can't be trusted but systems can as long as they are in place.

Recommendation: Be alert and ware of possible endeavors to cheat your business out of its well earned money. Don't trust people. Trust only systems. Don't trust people even if they are religious, volunteers, or community servants. These types of people have been known to commit fraud.

14　Credit

Lesson 35. Don't give credit to new buyers without a credit report.

Some firms have done this and have come to regret it. Some buyers like to buy on credit and then not pay their bills. Instead they take the merchandise and sell it and keep the money. Beware of this in your business. Don't trust anyone. Trust systems.

Recommendation: Some businesses are so desperate for new sales that they let anyone apply for credit and they get approved. You should do full and appropriate credit checks on all your buyers who want credit. Do not rush them through.

15   Credit Cards

Lesson 36. Don't assume that all credit card payments are for the business.

There have been many employers who have learned this lesson. I knew of a man who once got fired for not paying back personal expenses on his organization's credit card. Many people have been fired over this and many have been charged with embezzlement for misusing their organization's credit cards.

Recommendation: Ensure that a credit card report is done monthly reconciling their expenses to the report. Ask also for receipts for expenses over $ 25.

Lesson 37. Don't avoid having limits on credit cards.

Credit limits are good for they stop someone from going for months without reconciling their company's credit card. A summary reconciliation is a must for any employee who has a company credit card. It should accompany the request for payment before payment is made to the bank.

Recommendation: Reasonable limits should be put on all credit cards.

Lesson 38. Don't have credit cards unless you absolutely must.

Credit cards are generally bad news for companies. They should be avoided if they can or at least limited to the most important positions. A situation developed where an employee had a credit card and it went on for two years before reconciliation was done.

Recommendation: Attempt to get employees to sue their own credit cards and avoid the use of company cards.

16 Disgruntled Employees

Lesson 39. Don't ignore people who think they are owed by the company.

Some employees who have been an employee for years become disgruntled. They see bonuses going to managers and others whom they think do not deserve them. They look at their pay and believe that they are owed more than what they are receiving. Beware of disgruntled employees. This has been cited in many fraud and embezzlement cases as a reason why embezzlement was committed.

Recommendation: Many employees just want to be listened to and understood. Try this first. Try to explain why something has happened to them. Then keep an eye on their work.

17 Expense Reports

Lesson 40. Don't trust expense reports.

Employee expense reports should be inspected and management should make sure employees know that they are being scrutinized. Millions of dollars annually is probably taken illegally via expense reports. Mileage claims can be exaggerated. Expenses can be padded and trips can be falsified.

Recommendation: An astute supervisor should ask prying questions and if the employee gets annoyed he should watch that employee more closely. Receipts should be required for expenses at least over $ 25. But watch those under $ 25. It does not take long to cheat on a company expense report for claims under $ 25.

18 Expensive Gifts

Lesson 41. Don't ignore employees who buy expensive gifts for others.

Beware of employees who give expensive gifts. They may be doing it at your expense. The US Justice Department discovered that they were being defrauded thousands of dollars by a computer input clerk. This clerk would buy expensive gifts for the women in the office; such a diamond rings, with his new found wealth. He also purchased a home for his mother and a go-go bar in Washington DC. People became suspicious when he purchased expensive gifts.

Recommendation: Investigate any person who gives expensive gifts to others in the office.

19   Financial Explanations

Lesson 42. Don't necessarily believe financial explanations - be skeptical.

When people explain why they have new wealth (as to reasons why they have new cars or homes,) don't necessarily believe them. A school administrator, years ago, explained that his new found wealth was from receiving a substantial inheritance. Of course although it could have turned out not to be true.

Recommendation: When this type of thing happens in your organization be skeptical.

20   Fraud Policy

Lesson 43. Don't avoid having a fraud prevention policy.

A fraud prevention policy shows other employees that fraud is wrong and that it is okay for them to inform their boss of things that are unusual or irregular. It is sad that we have to have fraud policies to tell people that it is wrong to steal. But this is the age in which we live - the age of moral decline.

Recommendation: Develop a fraud policy and teach it to employees. Have a reward based system to encourage people to inform their supervisor or some other responsible person in the company of their suspicions.

21   Fraud Risk Assessment

Lesson 44. Don't think that a Fraud Risk Assessment (FRA) is not needed.

An FRA is important since it highlights any weak areas or areas of exposure to fraud and embezzlement. Wherever your firm is dealing with assets, money, revenues or secrets you want protected you need an FRA.

Recommendation: Implement an FRA as soon as is practicable. Cover all departments since every department has the opportunity to embezzle from the firm. If you need an example of an FRA consult the Appendix.

22   Gambling or Drugs

Lesson 45. Don't ignore employees with gambling problems.

Employees with gambling problems can be a huge risk for an organization. There have been numerous embezzlements that have taken place over the last thirty years to serve gambling habits. Some people have not intended to take the money permanently. They were intending to pay it back but it is well known that the house rarely loses. Usually the gambling catches up them eventually and they keep stealing hoping for that big payoff.

Recommendation: Employees' privacy must be guarded but if you come across any information that alerts you to an n employee having such a problem then keep an eye on that person's work.

Lesson 46. Don't ignore employees that have a drug problem.

Again, the same rule applies to these people as to the gamblers. Be aware of drug prone employees and have a policy which permits random drug tests. These tests could reveal more than a drug problem.

Recommendation: Have regular drug screenings on a surprise basis. Don't exempt anyone. If anyone has a drug problem get them help by referring them to a clinic.

23   Hiring

Lesson 47. Don't trust resumes when hiring.

There is so much lying on resumes you don't know what to believe and what not to. Some people lie on resumes, or at the very least exaggerate the truth. An exaggeration can be just as bad as lying since it can have the same consequences.

Recommendation: This is why it is good to utilize the services of an employment agency that have the time to check out potential employees thoroughly. It may end up costing more but will be worth it in the long run. Gaps in employment should be thoroughly investigated.

Lesson 48. Don't employ the first person to come along.

Be patient. Don't hire the first person that comes along that appears to have the qualification. Be sure to review the applications of a number of people who are qualified. This is especially important since so many felons have got out of jail and they go looking for jobs - usually in the field they know. Embezzlement felons usually receive anywhere from eighteen months to ten years incarceration and sometimes more than that but not often.

Recommendation: If it is legal where you live do a credit check and criminal background check on all potential employees.

Lesson 49. Don't trust someone because they are good looking.

Believe it or not this happens quite regularly. Just because someone knows how to dress they must be honest. So goes the sub-conscious logic. I can think of an example in a small professional office where the receptionist embezzled thousands of dollars. But the owners even thought about giving her a second chance because she was so nice.

Recommendation: Don't allow your appreciation of good looks to confuse your state of mind about hiring.

Lesson 50. Don't take reference phone numbers from resumes.

Look up reference phone numbers in the directory rather than take them off resumes. One man did this and had his friend on the other end of the phone giving him an excellent reference from a motel room.

Recommendation: If you can't find the number in the directory, ask the applicant for clarification. If she gives it and you, still call the number on the resume call it after hours and see what response you get.

Lesson 51. Don't permit hiring to be done outside HR or an employment agency.

If this is permitted then the wrong person could be hired. Sometimes managers like to go around the system and hire a person them-self. A friend or relative may need a job and the manager wants to hire them. This has happened n business but it is not a good practice. It could backfire on the hiring manager.

Recommendation: HR and employment agencies are used to hiring and used to the checks they employ to weed out unsuitable applicants. Use them to hire.

Lesson 52. Don't avoid hiring more qualified people.

Sometimes employers try to skimp on salaries and fail to attract the right people to the job. Hiring correctly can be critical to the firm's future. Truly evaluate the salary offered to ensure that it pays slightly above the average for that particular position.

Recommendation: Don't try to skimp on hiring the right person for the job. It will pay off.

Lesson 53. Don't avoid a credit check on the person you are about to hire.

A credit check could reveal a ton of debt. This is important if you are hiring for a financially responsible position. You would not want to hire someone who would want to steal from you.

Recommendation: Always have a credit check on new employees after receiving their permission. Tell them up front that when applying for a position with this firm a credit check will be required.

Lesson 54. Don't hire a convicted felon for a financially related job.

A criminal background check is important for financial positions and for any position in management. How would you like to have someone working as a bookkeeper who had spent five years in jail for embezzlement? Avoid this by having a criminal background check or a police report.

Recommendation: Be sure to get a criminal background check done before hiring new employees. Inform new applicants for positions that a criminal background check will be required as a condition of employment.

24 Human Resources

Lesson 55. Don't allow fraternization in the office.

Fraternization in the office can lead to collusion. This is also why nepotism policies are good. Nepotism is where a member of an existing employee's family is hired to work closely with the existing employee. Collusion is one of the most difficult forms of embezzlements to discover.

Recommendation: Inform staff that relatives or live in friends will not be employed in the same area within the company.

Tell them that they must inform the company if any new relationship is initiated.

Lesson 56. Don't forget to ask potential employees why they left last employer.

A lady who was fired from a California school district for embezzling half a million dollars tried to get a job at a bank. The astute interviewer recognized her name from newspaper reports and called the school district and asked "is this the person I have been reading about in the newspaper?" This bank ought to give the interviewer a medal.

Recommendation: Always ask new applicants why they left their last position. Get them to put this in writing on the application form for the position.

25   Information Technology

Lesson 57. Don't permit information to be attached to emails going out.

This is the way company secrets and confidential information gets out of your organization. Don't permit it at all levels. Clearly some have to have this function but not everyone should. Even those who are permitted to do this should have their files reviewed by a responsible person.

Recommendation: Write a policy and be sure to have all staff be aware of the policy forbidding attachments to be sent out without permission.

Lesson 58. Don't ignore the need for passwords to employee computers.

If this is not done other employees can get into computers and look for confidential information and company secrets. They can also send out emails from others computers and make it look as if it came from the person who usually uses that computer.

Recommendation: A policy should be established to make passwords mandatory on all computers and that no-one should share their password with anyone. Passwords should also be given up and changed as soon as people leave the employer and go to work somewhere else.

Lesson 59. Don't neglect having firewalls to detect emails with attachments.

Firewalls are important for ensuring that unwanted emails and web browsing is not taking place thus providing opportunity for employees to visit sits that will waste their time and company time. I heard of a man who worked on *eBay* most of the day on his employer's time - this is a form of embezzlement. But firewalls are also important for preventing intellectual property leaving the premises.

Recommendation: Programs can be purchase commercially that allow an employer to block access to certain web sites. A policy should be established banning visiting unauthorized web sites and informing them of the consequences for visiting such web sites. Employees should also be informed that a new program is being installed to forbid access to certain unauthorized web sites.

26   Intimidation

Lesson 60. Don't permit intimidation to close off questions.

One woman did this at a well known university. She was fierce with people and so people avoided her. All the time she was committing embezzlement. So anyone who had questions about what she was doing was intimidated by her manner and the embezzlement was not discovered for a long time.

Recommendation: Establish a company policy that forbids intimidation by one staff member to another.

27   Invoices

Lesson 61. Don't avoid checking invoices for fabrications of details.

Vendors and suppliers on occasion deliberately misstate the truth on invoices knowing that it might get through and be paid. Invoices should be looked at very closely and compare to the purchase order and the delivery docket (if one exists). Sometimes mistakes are also made causing the overall cost to increase.

Recommendation: All invoices should be checked by a reliable and trustworthy employee independent of the person who did the purchasing or the person who authorized the transaction.

Lesson 62. Don't trust invoices without back up.

If an invoice arrives unsolicited don't necessarily believe it. I have seen a number of invoices come in to an office for things that were never ordered. They are relying on the speed with which invoices are sometimes paid to get their unwarranted illegal gains.

Recommendation: Check every invoice for accuracy and that it has a corresponding purchase order.

28 Job Rotation

Lesson 63. Don't ignore the need for job rotation and back up.

This is very important to avoid embezzlement. It would have caught many past embezzlements. When an employee is moved out of a job into another job for a period of time the employee coming into the new jobs has a chance to come across something that is not right. If one employee suddenly leaves the employer then someone is trained to take over.

Recommendation: Establish a policy of job rotation for all staff. Along with this have a mandatory vacation policy where everyone is required to take off at least two weeks per year. Inform them that someone else will be doing their job while they are gone.

29 Late Notices

Lesson 64. Don't ignore delinquent or late notices.

Receiving late notices regularly could indicate that checks intended for certain payees are not getting to them. Thus, embezzlement could be found to be occurring in the organization. This is why a manager needs to receive the mail and not give anyone the opportunity to pull things out of the mail and dispose of them.

Recommendation: Evaluate all late notices and have someone else other than the payables person look into every late notice.

30   Logical Questions

Lesson 65. Don't stop asking "why do we need to ...?"

This question was asked and it was why a very large embezzlement was found. Collusion was involved and they had set up their own employment agency and were approving bills for non-existent temporary workers. So ask questions and try to get logical answers.

Recommendation: Questions are sometimes a way to unravel fraud. Keep asking logical questions. You never know when you will hit upon something significant.

31   Longevity of Employment

Lesson 66. Don't think long term employees are honest.

This is one of the greatest risks to your firm or organization. Most embezzlers have been employed for long periods of time. They have gained the trust of their employers by working so many years for them. In fact, the average length of time the embezzler has been employed is around eight years. So don't give blind trust to people just because they have been with you for a long period of time.

Recommendation: Treat long-term employees the same as any other. Don't relax internal controls around them. The average employee who commits embezzlement has been at the job for eight years.

33

32 Mail

Lesson 67. Don't permit mail to be opened by just one employee.

Having more than one employee opening the mail makes it more difficult for employees to take things out of the mail such as checks, late notices and statements.

Recommendation: Establish a policy that makes it always necessary to have two employees present when opening mail. One should not be supervised by the other. They should be equals.

33 Management Overrides

Lesson 68. Don't permit management to override established systems

This occasionally happens only to leave the entity with less security than it had before. Management overrides are dangerous since they involve violating systems, policies and procedures put in place for a reason. When that is violated it opens up the company for embezzlement.

Recommendation: Establish a policy that forbids management overrides of internal controls and reports any overrides to the owners of the business.

34 Payroll

Lesson 69. Don't allow employees to calculate their own remuneration.

Recently one man got charged with embezzlement for doing just this. He was hired with the understanding that he would receive a salary and a percentage of debts that he collected. He was supposed to get 30% of every debt he collected. He thought it would be nice to have 30% of all revenues and so that is precisely what he did.

Recommendation: Always have someone verify a calculation made by any employee as to what pay they receive.

Lesson 70. Don't leave payroll checks unsecured.

Payroll checks are like gold to some people. They must not be left unsecured for people to help themselves. This brings in obvious risks to the organization. Sometimes they are left in a storage room without being secured. This is not good internal control.

Recommendation: Payroll checks should be kept under lock and key in a secure place.

Lesson 71. Don't assume employees who left employment are not being paid.

This is an embezzlement caused by payroll employees. When a person is not taken off the payroll - guess what? - checks still get printed. This can be particularly bad as unauthorized pays can amount to substantial sums over a period of time.

Recommendation: Due diligence should be applied to this type of thing to ensure no illegal payments are made. Management checking is necessary to be sure that no unauthorized payments are being made.

Lesson 72. Don't avoid having surprise payroll audits.

Surprise payroll audits are great to detect and prevent embezzlement. A surprise payroll audit involves handing out all pay checks to employees and having them come in to a central location and sign for their pay. All missing employees need to be accounted for and they need to come in and collect their pay in person at a later time if they cannot come in at the time of the audit.

Recommendation: Have a policy that tells people in advance that you will have surprise payroll audits occur from time to time. When performing this audit ensure that all payroll checks are picked up personally by the employee within a reasonable time period.

Lesson 73. Don't trust what you have commonly seen.

A Controller for an oil related company added substantial sums of money to her pay check and then deducted the same amount in the form of extra tax payments, therefore showing the net as the same as it always has been.

Recommendation: This actually happened and so a complete check of payroll including a review of gross amounts is necessary to avoid being ripped off by this crime.

Lesson 74. Don't think that all pay checks are made to legitimate employees.

You only want legitimate employees to be paid. Ghost employees are employees with made up names that don't exist.

Recommendation: Therefore, it is appropriate that someone responsible occasionally look for ghost employees in the payroll records. But make sure that they are the real patrol records and not made up fictional records.

35   Petty Cash

Lesson 75. Don't sign off on petty cash vouchers without receipts.

Petty cash is necessary to enable the purchase of small supplies. Original receipts are necessary to avoid bogus claims against petty cash. One man got away with a million dollars out of petty cash.

Recommendation: The receipts should have what was purchased and the amount that matches the claim. Ensure that they are not duplicate receipts. Initial each one presented with a unique signature so that you know if it is presented again.

Don't permit photocopies of receipts since the original invoice or receipt can be used again.

Lesson 76. Don't avoid having a custodian of petty cash.

There needs to be a custodian of petty cash and preferably two custodians to avoid money going missing or fraudulent claims being submitted. Sometimes petty cash custodians think it is alright to borrow from the fund. It is best not to allow this and to have a policy against it.

Recommendation: Someone must be in charge of petty cash. Preferably it should be handled by two people to avoid "borrowing" from it.

Lesson 77. Don't avoid having surprise cash counts of petty cash.

Surprise petty cash counts can reveal things that would raise your eye brows. Records not being complete, missing cash and other irregularities can be discovered with a surprise cash count.

Recommendation: Surprise cash counts can reveal a lot and catch unsuspecting employees. Don't let them attempt to delay you from looking at the cash and the receipts.

36   Printed Reports

Lesson 78. Don't always believe printed reports.

Printed reports although looking official and valid can be totally false and give a misleading picture of what is really going on.

Recommendation: If they are not computer generated insist on a computer generated report of the general ledger or other item in the general ledger. Don't accept delays - delays can be used to get your mind off your request. Always look at reports with skepticism even if they are computer generated. Look at reports with a logical common sense approach.

37   Purchase Orders

Lesson 79. Don't avoid doing a sequence check of all purchased orders.

Purchase orders can be used to buy things on credit. They can be used illegally without the employer's permission. For example, they can be used by a department manager to buy things that they can later resell. While in the meantime the employer pays the bills for what they thought were valid purchases.

Recommendation: It is good to keep purchase orders under lock and key and to perform sequence checks on them to see if any are missing.

38   Religious Employees

Lesson 80. Don't think religious employees will never defraud you.

At the fraud research center we have noticed that there is no special advantage to having a religious employee. Churches have been ripped off for millions by some of their religious employees. The latest case indicates that a bookkeeper for a large church embezzled more than $2 million. Recently a religious woman was the suspect of a fraud.

Recommendation: Treat all employees the same and hold them all to the same standards.

39   Retiree Payments

Lesson 81. Don't assume that all retiree payments are valid.

If you have a retirement program of some kind don't assume all withdrawals are valid. An administrator can easily forge a signature and change an address to a more convenient address in order to steal funds. By doing this it could take years to discover. Also if a person dies who has retired without drawing on the retirement funds it may never be found without a thorough audit.

Recommendation: Have an audit of retiree payments. Also have a policy that ensures double verification. That is, someone should always sign off on changes to retiree details and outgoing payments.

Lesson 82. Don't avoid sending a letter to retirees confirming a distribution.

When a retiree lodges a form to withdraw funds a confirmation letter should be sent to them by a different employee who received the form and a different employee who would distribute the funds.

Recommendation: Have a policy that ensures a letter is sent to the retired employee that they are making a withdrawal of assets. Provided the correct address is on file, this may catch a potential fraudulent distribution.

40   Returned Goods

Lesson 83. Don't allow goods returned by same people who purchased them.

This type of thing can lead to embezzlement and fraud. It will occur to them eventually that if they purchased and then returned goods they could possibly pocket the cash, if cash is given for returned goods.

Recommendation: It is important to not have the same person return goods that purchased them in the first place. If this is too difficult to administer then at least insist on receiving the invoice before the goods go back, copy it and then keep a file on returned goods with the photocopies of the salient invoices.

41   Segregation of Duties

Lesson 84. Don't avoid segregation of duties.

This is very difficult for some small entities to do due to the cost. But if you can't afford to hire more staff to segregate certain things then you need to make sure that you take away the most important things from one person and do them yourself. For example, the person who does the bank reconciliation and the posting to the general ledger should not write any checks them-self. There have been many embezzlements where too much control was given to a bookkeeper or office manager who proceeded to rip off the employer.

Recommendation: Have a policy of the segregation of duties. Don't let it slip and fall into anything goes. This is a big danger with small companies. Managers don't have a lot of time to check on internal controls. Therefore, professional assistance should be utilized.

42   Short Loading

Lesson 85. Don't ignore possibility of collusive or non-collusive short loading.

This is a viable method of embezzling goods and money from an employer. Short loading is billing a customer for goods not delivered or under-delivered. Such deliveries can add up quickly to hundreds of thousands of dollars.

Recommendation: Make sure your receiving staff are competent and honest. Double check certain deliveries to ensure that everything supposed to be delivered is in fact delivered.

43   Supplies

Lesson 86. Don't assume all purchased supplies are used by your firm.

Many an organization has found that they were not the recipient of supplies that they had purchased through a "trusted" employee. One such person recently thought he had gotten away with a substantial number of valuable computer parts until he was caught. He was ordering supplies and then selling them again.

Recommendation: Keep your eye open for supplies that you have paid for. Establish a double check system of doing an inventory count of supplies. This should be done especially for valuable supplies purchased.

44 Surveillance

Lesson 87. Don't avoid surveillance on employees accepting cash.

Cameras on people who have a job of collecting cash have paid off for some employers. If you have a business that is heavy on the cash think about using surveillance cameras. If some employees are desperate enough they will still take the cash but at least they will be photographed in the act.

Recommendation: Where you have large amounts of cash passing over a counter it is important to have surveillance cameras watching.

Lesson 88. Don't ignore surveillance of employees at the cash register.

They could scan another code instead of the one for the goods being purchased. This could be done for friends and relatives. The cash register is a pivotal lace to embezzle. If someone comes through who is a friend of the cashier the cashier could easily take out a lower priced bar code and pass it through the register as if it were the bar code on the product being purchased.

Recommendation: Watch cash employees very carefully.

45 Temporary Employees

Lesson 89. Don't trust temporary employees.

If you must use temporary employees use them for non conse-
quential duties until they have worked there for quite a while.
Then later, if they are put on jobs that are more important that
have risks associated with them, then ensure that controls are
in place to avoid embezzlement. *HP* learned this lesson the
hard way.

Recommendation: Don't put temporary employees on large
dollar items or activities. Use them on the mundane work
needed and utilize full-time regular employees for the high
cost or valuable transactions.

46 Too Big

**Lesson 90. Don't think that since you are big firm that you
will be fraud-free.**

There have been many big companies, public agencies and
non-profits that have had frauds and embezzlements. Never
rest on your laurels and think that it can't happen to your entity.

Recommendation: It can happen and may be happening right
now under your nose without your knowledge. You must insist on strong internal controls as much as is plausible and
possible having regard to your business circumstances.

47 Too Much Control

Lesson 91. Don't give too much control.

This is similar to not enough segregation of duties. When people are employed in small companies they are given way too much control of almost everything. For example, when a new bookkeeper is hired they are oftentimes given the check book, the responsibility for the general ledger, the bank statements and bank reconciliation not to mention petty cash, accounts receivable and accounts payable. This is just way too much control. There are too many opportunities to commit fraud.

Recommendation: Limit control to one of a few things but not too many or all activities of the office.

48 Trust

Lesson 92. Don't trust anyone - trust established systems.

When trust is given you might as well give up your business. Time and time again trust has been broken even by the most trusted employees. People have embezzled who are church going, family oriented people, community servants, and they look good and talk well.

Recommendation: But trust should only be given to systems in so far as they are installed and are working.

49   Unusual Employee Behavior

Lesson 93. Don't avoid looking for unusual signs of employee behavior.

Nervousness, drug habits, gambling, buying expensive gifts for office staff or family members, staying late and never taking vacations can all be signs that something is wrong. Not in all cases but usually in some. We at the Fraud Research center have noticed this in the study of all the cases that come into us that these are all warning signs that something is not quite right.

Recommendation: Be alert to unusual behavior characteristics. These could be signs of fraud.

50   Vacations

Lesson 94. Don't allow financial employees to avoid vacations.

Some people never take vacations. Watch those people. A reason that they may not be taking vacations / holidays is that they are afraid of being caught in a crime. When they are gone usually someone else does their job for them and the concern is that they may find out when doing the job that the person had been embezzling funds.

Recommendation: You should insist on financial employees taking vacations. If they complain don't listen to them - tell them that they must go and if they do not pick the time when they will go, you will.

51   Variance Analysis

Lesson 95. Don't avoid variance analyses of actual to budget.

When embezzlers take money they have to record it somewhere and that somewhere is usually the general ledger. So after you have done the budget for the forthcoming year compare the actual expenses with the budget and see if there are any large variances (differences).

Recommendation: Variance analysis should be done by a responsible employee that has no cash or check responsibilities but that has understanding of the business. If there significant variances they should be investigated and explanations demanded. If the answers are not satisfactory from the person who did the investigation, they should be looked into by another person.

52 Vendors

Lesson 96. Don't permit new suppliers without a new vendor request form.

Employers have a need to do business with new vendors on a regular basis. Vendors are important for businesses to get the supplies they need to operate their business. But "alleged" new vendors can be used to rip off thousands if not millions from a company.

Recommendation: Having a buyer fill out a new vendor request form protects the business from an embezzler trying to set up a dummy vendor to whom they can make payments. This takes extra work but it is worth every minute of it. To fill it out will only take a few minutes and it makes anyone considering setting up a dummy vendor to think twice before embarking on this type of project.

53 Wealth

Lesson 97. Don't believe the stories of sudden explained or unexplained employee wealth.

Many a prospering employee has been found later to have been embezzling from their employer. Don't be naive and believe every word that is spoken. Some people may be telling the truth but some may not.

Recommendation: You need to be skeptical when you see an employee with signs of new wealth.

54 Whistle-blowers

Lesson 98. Don't make it difficult for whistle-blowers.

Don't make whistle-blowers comments seem unimportant or silly. This sort of behavior needs to be encouraged not discouraged. Many embezzlements and frauds against employers have been discovered by whistle-blowers. This is despite the fact that those same companies had audits. Whistle-blowers need to feel comfortable when they report suspicious activities. They need to feel that you will take them seriously if they come forward.

Recommendation: Establish a policy supporting whistle blowers and offering rewards for doing so.

Lesson 99. Don't be unrewarding toward employees who want to report.

You should reward those who come forward with information that leads to the discovery of a fraud.

Recommendation: Establish a policy to reward a reporting employee. It could be taking off a day with pay, a sum of money, becoming employee of the month, or some other desirable benefit that is unique to your business.

55 Wire Transfers

Lesson 100. Don't assume all wire transfers are for the benefit of your entity.

Wire transfers are one of the least controlled aspects of a business. They are usually done by a high ranking manager who has sole authority over the wiring of funds to other bank accounts. He or she could easily set up a bank account and wire funds into it if adequate and strong controls are not in place. Another thing that has been done is forging of a counter-signature on wiring instructions. This does not happen very often but when it happens it is usually quite a large embezzlement.

Recommendation: Have two people sign off on wire transfers.

Lesson 101. Don't neglect to have bank phone back a wire transfer order.

Occasionally firms need to do wire transfers within the banking system. This can be particularly dangerous for a company if one person is charged with this responsibility. After a while an employee may think that they can wore money anywhere. This has happened.

Recommendation: You should always have a system set up that enables the bank to call another person in the wiring organization to confirm the wire. This is one of the best controls to have in place to avoid embezzlement of business funds. Make sure the bank understands that no-one wiring funds has the authority to change the system that is set up to avoid mal-wiring.

Thou shalt not steal.
Exodus 20:15

www.ingramcontent.com/pod-product-compliance
Lightning Source LLC
Chambersburg PA
CBHW071813170526
45167CB00003B/1289